wonders of
Measurement

D1356379

Hittite relief representing the act of weighing

Wonders of
MEASUREMENT

OWEN S. LIEBERG

BAILEY BROTHERS & SWINFEN LIMITED
Folkestone

To J.A.D.

Photographs are reproduced through the courtesy of: Alnor Instrument Company, 49; BOAC, 61 (top left); British Museum, copyright reserved, 2,4, 19, 24; *The Daily Telegraph,* London, 61 (third from top, right); Ford of Britain, 61 (second from top, right); Kent Meters Ltd., 21; Moore & Wright (Sheffield) Ltd., 66; Musée du Louvre, Paris; Frontispiece; NASA, 71,72 (top); National Bureau of Standards, Department of Commerce, Frontispiece, 14, 36, 68; National Physical Laboratory, England, Crown Copyright reserved, (right), 12, 26, 39, 69; The Science Museum, London, 67; Sifam Electrical Instrument Company, 43; The Smithsonian Institution, 25 (bottom), 27 (bottom); Streeter Collection, Yale Medical Library, 29. Diagrams by Owen S. Lieberg.

Published in Great Britain by Bailey Brothers and Swinfen Ltd.,

Copyright © 1976 by Owen S.Lieberg
All rights reserved
No part of this book may be reproduced in any form
without permission in writing from the publisher

SBN 561 00214 2

Printed by Clarke, Doble & Brendon Ltd, Plymouth

Contents

Photograph of reflections of a laser beam used in measuring carbon monoxide.

1 The story of Measurement

Have you ever thought what life would be like without measurement? No miles, no kilometres, no metres, no clocks or watches to tell the time, no pints, no litres, no weights, no money, no way to indicate the length or width of a piece of wood or the size of a ball. We depend on measurement for almost everything we do — in science and engineering, in commerce and farming, in the factory and at home. It is so commonplace that we seldom realise how important it is. To us in the twentieth century, life and communication are inseparable. If we could not communicate, life as we know it could not go on. In order to communicate we need measurement.

In prehistoric times, when people lived in caves, there was no need to measure. To eat, a man had to hunt or fish, but he would have found it difficult to tell others how far he had gone or how many fish he had caught. Accuracy was not his problem.

Later, as men began to live in groups, there was a necessity to communicate, to tell others where there was a river with

Assyrian lion weight dating from the eighth century B.C.

fish, or how many animals had been seen at a water hole. All the primitive hunter could do was spread his hands apart for size or point to his fingers or toes for numbers.

Often the groups were nomadic tribes, moving from place to place, hunting or following herds of cattle or sheep. The Sumerians, for instance, settled in Mesopotamia more than 6,000 years ago and began cultivating the fertile soil and raising crops. They no longer moved about, but settled in villages, and the villages grew into walled towns. Agriculture created a new age, and with it, the beginnings of civilization.

With civilization, there was a real need for measuring. The early farmers brought products to market for barter and trading. Men began to depend on each other's labours. Farms had to be marked off, houses had to be built, irrigation systems had to be laid out. Numbers and counting were only a start. A standard of comparison was needed — something

2

that could be seen and that was unvarying. Units for weighing and measuring were the only answer. Traders could see weights, scales could be balanced, and lengths could be compared.

In those early days of civilization, the ruling classes were priestly skywatchers. Astronomers and astrologers kept calendar records and devised numbering systems to solve the bartering problems. The Sumerians, and later the Babylonians, used a system that was partly sexagesimal, or multiples of six, and partly decimal, or multiples of ten — 1, 6, 10, 60, 100, 360, and so on. The decimal system may have been derived from the ten fingers and toes, but the sexagesimal numbering came, it is almost certain, from the oldest geometrical measurement of antiquity that has survived without change for thousands of years — "the degree of arc."

This is shown in Figure 1. The arc of a circle enclosed by a chord the same length as the radius is always equal to one-

When the chord of a circle equals the radius there will always be six chords in that circle and the angle will be one-sixth of 360 degrees.

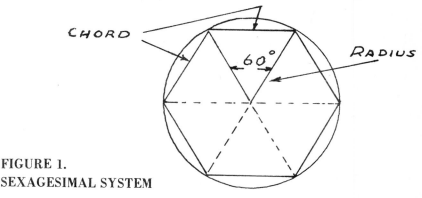

FIGURE 1.
SEXAGESIMAL SYSTEM

sixth of the circumference of the circle. If the angle opposite this arc is reckoned at 60 degrees, a circle therefore contains 360 degrees at its centre.

Such a division of a circle was very useful. Any circle could be divided into 60 minutes, and those minutes into 60 seconds. These early people reckoned the year as 360 days,

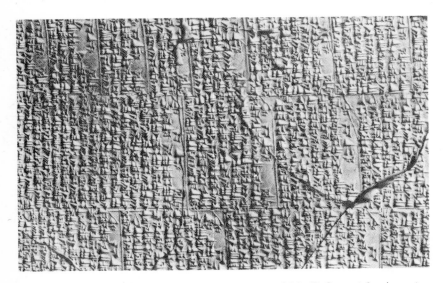

Portion of cuneiform clay tablet, from 1800 B.C., with Assyrian mathematical calculations. Side view shows curved profile and shape of tablet.

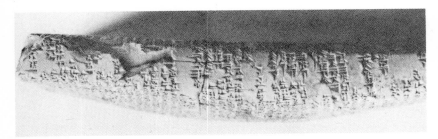

and even today, measurements of time and of the earth — another circle — are counted in degrees.

Such calculations eventually led to the science of mathematics. Early inhabitants of the lands of the Middle East knew how to solve equations, calculate square roots, and determine the areas of circles. How do we know? From archaeologists who have uncovered thousands of clay tablets on which were inscribed historical records and mathematical solutions in cuneiform, the oldest known form of writing. Cuneiform means wedge-shaped. Figure 2 shows how the Sumerians wrote numbers. Using a stylus, they cut the symbols into a clay tablet when it was still wet, then baked it in the sun.

Other early civilizations devised their own numbering systems. The Egyptians developed the decimal system of tens. The Greeks were the first to use the duodecimal system of dividing units into twelfths, and the Romans, rising in power, copied the Greeks.

With such a knowledge of numbers, measuring could be done with a degree of refinement. Instead of being limited to counting fingers or toes, standards of measurement came into

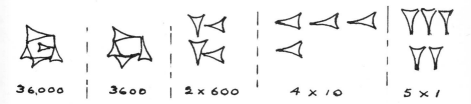

FIGURE 2. SUMERIAN SYMBOLS

These symbols showing numbering and addition, are taken from a clay tablet written over 4,000 years ago.

5

use. Vessels could be made to measure grain or liquids by quantity; farm produce could be counted and weighed. Eventually, traders began to carry silver bars instead of bulky sacks of goods, and in time the silver bars were replaced by small discs of silver and the world had its first money.

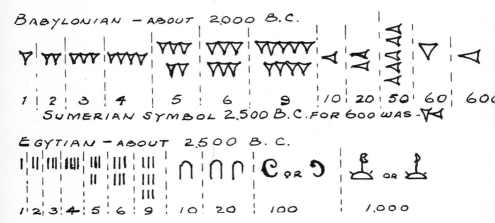

FIGURE 3. ANCIENT NUMBERING SYMBOLS

Today, accurate measurement is itself a science, the science of *metrology*. It is divided into six basic sections: (a) length, (b) mass, (c) time, (d) temperature, (e) light or luminosity, and (f) electricity. Metrology links all branches of science together in the measurement and interpretation of observed facts. Measurement is comparison with a known standard — something we can see or touch or record by a measuring device. To measure is to know.

2   Length

The earliest unit of measurement and one that goes far back into antiquity is the *cubit*. It is not certain who originated the cubit. The Sumerians, the ancient Egyptians, the Babylonians, and the Hebrews all used it as the prime unit of length, as did many nomadic tribes that lived in the Middle East. It was a simple measurement, the distance between the elbow and the tip of the middle finger. Naturally, it varied from man to man and from country to country, being about 44.7 centimetres to over 50 centimetres.

According to hieroglyphic symbols carved on their monuments and on clay tablets, the Egyptians had a short cubit just under 45 centimetres in length and a longer, or royal, cubit which was about 52 centimetres. It is not surprising therefore that during the building of the First Pyramid, about 2,500 B.C., they were using cubit measuring rods to enable them to measure distances with remarkable precision. The builders of the gigantic Cheops Pyramid at Giza were extremely accurate. Using only cubit rods and other crude devices such as knotted ropes and a plumb line (a cord with a

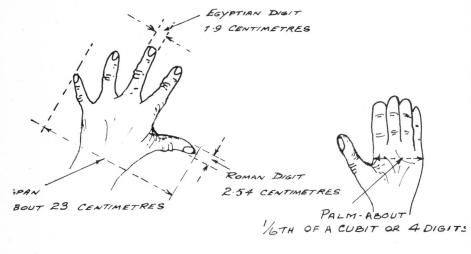

EGYPTIAN DIGIT
1·9 CENTIMETRES

ROMAN DIGIT
2·54 CENTIMETRES

SPAN
BOUT 23 CENTIMETRES

PALM-ABOUT
1/6TH OF A CUBIT OR 4 DIGITS

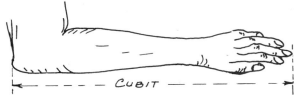

CUBIT

FIGURE 4. EARLY BODY MEASUREMENTS

Early measurements were taken from average sized human limbs. One hand equalled approximately 10 centimetres.

lead weight on one end to test the perpendicular of a wall or doorway), each of the four sides of the square base were, within a few centimetres, exactly the same length — 230.4 metres.

One Egyptian measuring rod, found at Thebes in Upper Egypt, was hinged at the centre to fold like a modern carpenter's rule. It was one royal cubit in length and divided into units of seven *palms*, the palm being the width of the four fingers of the hand. The seventh palm of this rod was subdivided into four units called *digits*, each being equal to the breadth of the middle finger — approximately 1.9 centimetres. Some of the digits were again divided into smaller divisions.

Another unit used by the Egyptians was the *span*, the distance between the tip of the thumb and the little finger of the outstretched hand — between 20 and 23 centimetres.

To make the base of a pyramid an accurate square with right angles of 90 degrees, the Egyptians drew a dividing line between two markers on the ground, as shown in Figure 5. With two pegs attached to a cord, one in the ground by the marker and one free to swing, an arc was drawn (AB). By moving the peg to the second marker and swinging the free peg in the opposite direction another arc (CD) intersected the first. The line drawn between the two intersecting points crossed the original line at right angles.

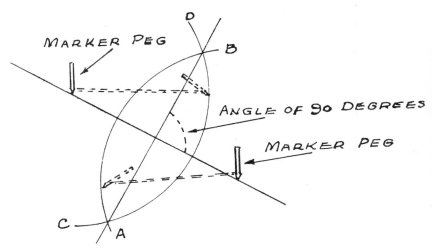

FIGURE 5. MAKING A RIGHT ANGLE

Early Egyptian method of making a right angle on the ground.

There are many references to measurement in the Bible. The cubit was the unit of length used when Noah built his ark and King Solomon his temple. There was also the *fathom*, from the Greek *faden* meaning "spread". It was the unit of the leadsman on a ship as he measured the depth of water alongside. He would throw a rope, with a stone or a piece of lead attached, into the sea and as he pulled up the rope he would measure it by counting off lengths of his outstretched arms. The fathom today is still 6 feet, (1.83 metres approximately).

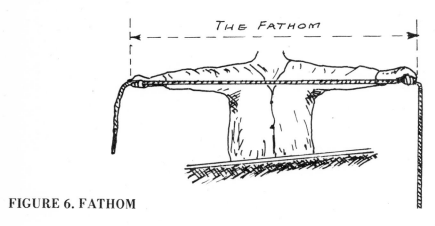

FIGURE 6. FATHOM

The *furlong*, or furrow long, was the length of a furrow that oxen would plough in a common field, which was regarded as a square containing 10 acres. It measured about one-fifth of a kilometre.

Eventually the *foot* replaced the cubit as a common measure. The foot was used extensively by the Romans, and the Roman foot was subdivided into twelve parts or *unciae*, from which, in time, came the word *inch*. (An inch, at first, was a

FIGURE 7.
ROMAN PACE OR STRIDE

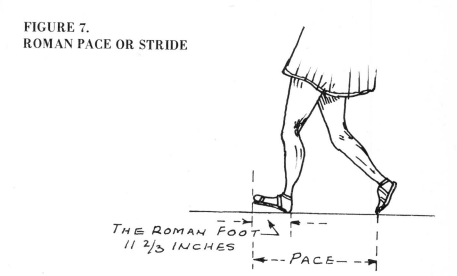

THE ROMAN FOOT
11 2/3 INCHES
PACE

hand measurement, the width of a man's thumb.)

The Romans gave us the *mile*, from their *mille passuum*, literally a thousand of paces. They reckoned the pace or stride as the average distance — 5 feet — between lifts of the same foot. This, in Roman times, became the English mile of 5,000 feet. Centuries later, to standardize the mile with agricultural measurements, Queen Elizabeth 1 decreed it to be 8 furlongs or 5,280 feet. In measuring fields or surveying land, it was more convenient to have a mile equal to eight times a furlong which was 660 feet.

Throughout the Middle Ages, many different systems of measurement had spread across Europe. They had become so changed and modified in usage from the original Sumerian, Egyptian, and Roman, that by the end of the eighteenth century, scientists were beginning to become dissatisfied with the different units. Every country had varying measures, or the same unit meant different things.

France had so many different measurements — nearly every community having its own — that the leaders of the French Revolution of 1790, finding distasteful anything having to do with the old monarchy and urged by the scientists to bring uniformity to the existing confusion, swept the old French standards away and substituted a new and simple system of measurement which they called *metric*.

Here was an easy system based on decimal numbering — that is, multiplying or dividing by ten. Its basic or primary unit was the *metre*, which came from the Greek *metron* or measure, and was equal to one ten-millionth part of the distance between the North Pole and the equator on a line running through Paris. The metre is equal to 39.37 inches.

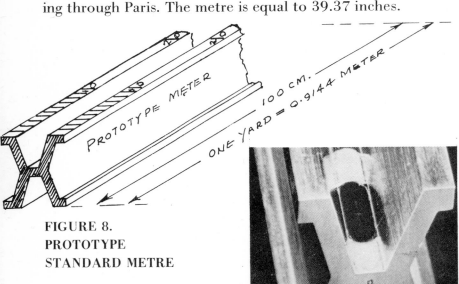

FIGURE 8.
PROTOTYPE
STANDARD METRE

**French prototype metre bar
showing wing-shaped design.**

The French, when deciding on the metre as the basic unit, subdivided it into centimetres and millimetres for smaller measurements of length – 2.54 centimetres being equal to one inch. Using the same decimal principle for longer measurement, 1.000 metres was called a *kilometre* – 1,609 kilometres equalled 1 mile.

The metric system was quickly adopted by other countries and soon became firmly established throughout Europe with the exception of Great Britain. It later spread to several South American countries.

While this was happening in France, George Washington, in his first Presidential message to Congress in 1790, stressed the necessity of ". . . uniformity in currency, weights and measures." At about the same time, Thomas Jefferson proposed that the United States should also adopt the metric or decimal system. But his suggestion was turned down by Congress, leaving the United States and Great Britain to retain the yard and its irregular system of measurement.

To make these two standards, the yard and the metre, compare visually to a definite measurement, international units were adopted at the International Metric Convention in May, 1875. Today, in the United States a bar of platinum-iridium alloy with two lines engraved on it exactly a yard apart is stored in an air-conditioned vault at the National Bureau of Standards in Washington. The French International Prototype Metre, kept at Sçvres near Paris, has a special shape of a winged cross section to give it rigidity.

Although at the time of writing the United States has not officially adopted the metre, it was legalized by an Act of Congress in 1866 but not made obligatory. During the next decade, it seems certain that all the English-speaking count-

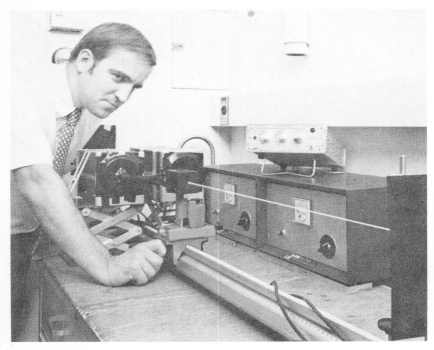

Methane-helium-neon laser beam apparatus for measuring lengths with an accuracy of one part in a hundred thousand million.

ries will follow the rest of the world and change over to the metric system, abolishing the yard, the quart, the pint, the bushel, and the other non-metric measurements. It is already widely used. To give an instant visual comparison between inch and centimetre, most rulers have inches marked on one edge and centimetres on the opposite.

Length, or linear measurement, is also used to determine the area — the extent of surface — of a square or rectangle or any other geometrical figure. Area is given in square inches, square feet, square centimetres, square metres, and so on. The areas of some geometrical figures, such as a square with equal sides, are easy to find by simply multiplying the width by the length. Other areas are not so easy to determine. The circle, for instance, has two quite different measurements, its radius — or half its diameter — and its circumference, or the distance around its outer edge. By dividing the diameter into the circumference, the result is always the same, no matter how large or small is the circle. It is always 3.1416, or approximately $3^{1}/_{7}$. This number is called *pi* — written as the Greek letter π — and is the ratio or relationship of the circumference of a circle to its diameter. The area of a circle is found by multiplying *pi* (3.1416) by radius × radius, that is, $\pi \ \tau^2$. We call this *pi* τ squared.

Today, when an accurate unvarying standard of length is essential for scientific work, physicists use a new method of determining it exactly. Following a suggestion by a Frenchman, Jacques Babinet, in 1872, it was discovered that when the element Krypton-86 is heated in a vacuum, 1,650,763.73 of its pulsating waves of orange-red light are exactly equal to one metre. Since it is accurate to one part in 100 million and can be reproduced in scientific laboratories throughout the world, this defining of the metre has now been adopted by International Convention as the universal standard and unit of length for a related yard and metre. One yards equals 0.9144 of a metre.

However, since the Krypton-86 length standard is not perfect because it cannot be used directly to measure long distances, a new laser technique has been found to give precise length measurement of extremely high stability and accuracy. This laser wave length promises to be nearly 1,000 times as reproducible as the present Krypton-86 length standard. The laser may therefore soon replace the element

Krypton-86 for defining the metre and then will doubtless be adopted internationally.

3   Capacity

Turning back again to that cradle of civilization, the Middle East, the satisfactory use of units of length soon led to other demands. People needed a unit of volume or cubic capacity for liquid measure when bartering or selling wine and olive oil. From the land of Sumer and Babylon, cuneiform symbols disclose the use of linear measurements as the basis for cubic volume. We use the word "cubic" to mean three-dimensional. Units of volume are the cubic inch, cubic foot, cubic centimetre, and so on.

To determine capacity — how much a container will hold — you multiply the length by the width by the height. One *hand-breadth* in each of the three directions gave the Babylonians their liquid measure which they called the *ka*. At about the same time the early Egyptians were using the cubic cubit to give them their *khar* and *hin*. The *hin* was equal to about half a litre of our measure, while the *khar* was nearly 100 litres.

The early Hebrews had a *kor* and a *hin*, their *kor* being about 360 litres and their *hin* about 6 litres. For smaller measure they used the *log*, a little less than half a litre. They also had the *bath*, nearly 36 litres. In the Bible we read " . . . . ten acres of vineyard shall yield one bath." The Hebrews also had a special unit of capacity, which was associated with their religion, the sacred *bath* equal to just over 29 litres.

In those far-off days, about 4,000 years ago, it must have been very difficult for travellers in Egypt, Babylonia, and other Middle Eastern lands where countries and communities had different standards for dry and liquid measures. Some merchants had one measure for purchasing and one for selling. Traders had to carry several sets of measuring vessels to meet the different requirements of the towns they were visiting. And there were sometimes unusual containers to get acquainted with. During excavations in Pompeii, it was discovered that some of the smaller bowls, used for liquids, were emptied by removing a plug from a hole in the bottom.

The ancient Greeks had for centuries been greatly influenced by the Babylonian system of measurement. They also used linear measurements to calculate capacity or liquid volume. Their primary unit for liquids was the *metretes*, about 39 litres. They subdivided the *metretes* into twelve small units, called *amphora*, equal to about 3 litres. The name was later given to the two-handled jars — called *amphorae* — many of which have been recovered in recent years from wrecked Greek ships in the Mediterranean.

The Romans copied the Greeks in many of their liquid measurements, using the same terminology but with different volumes. They, too, had a unit of capacity called the *amphora*, but the Roman *amphora* was much larger, equal to nearly 26½ litres. When Europe fell under Roman domina-

17283111

This storage jar for wine, found in Nimrud, is about 2,500 years old.

tion, their basic units of measurement soon became the sole system for those European countries.

French influence in the eighth and ninth centuries brought new measures of capacity to the western world. Although the French transported wine by the *muid* — their standard wine cask of a little over 270 litres — they had two small measures for selling liquids, the *pot* and the *quatre*, used particularly

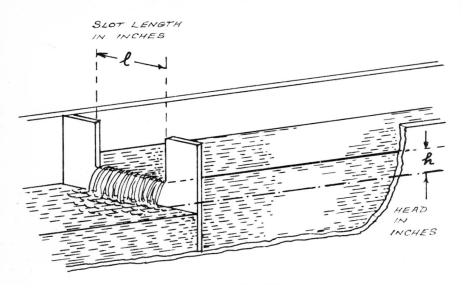

FIGURE 9. MEASURING WATER FLOW

One method of measuring the quantity of water flowing in a stream or canal is by the use of weirs or dams.

for wine and beer. The quatre, from which we get our word quart, was one-fourth of the pot and equal to between 1½ and 2 litres.

It varied in different parts of France. The French *velte* was ¹⁄₃₆ part of a muid, and a half-*velte* was the *galon*, from which we get our word, gallon.

In the thirteenth and fourteenth centuries Britain had its wine cask, the *tun* of 252 gallons, and had adopted the gallon as its smaller and primary unit of capacity, but it varied according to use. When Elizabeth became queen, in 1558, there were three different gallons — the ale gallon of 282 cubic inches, a corn gallon of 272 cubic inches, and the wine gallon of 231 cubic inches — which caused considerable argument over which measure to use for tax purposes.

By the year 1700, the English inns and drinking places had

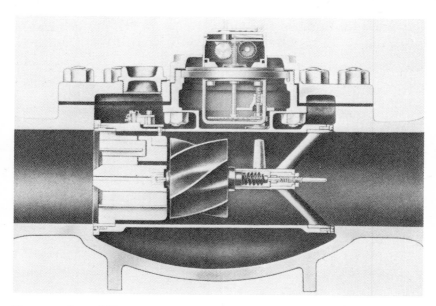

Cross section of flow meter in pipe.

so reduced the size of the wine gallon and, consequently, the tankards and pots, that a legal quantity had to be set by Parliament. In that year the British wine gallon was finally defined as ". . . a round vessel containing 231 cubic inches."

In the American colonies, the British wine gallon was

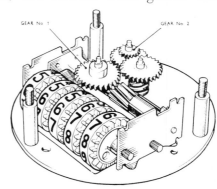

Direct reading counter used on mechanical meters such as the flow meter above.

popular, but there were many variations in the size of the gallon and bushel. After the War of Independence, uniformity was essential for trade. With different measures of volume from state to state, many arguments ensued which continued until 1830 when Congress appointed a Swiss immigrant, Ferdinand Hassler, who was teaching mathematics at West Point, to investigate the problem. Six years later his recommendations were adopted by Congress and the U.S. gallon legalized at 231 cubic inches for liquid measure, the same as the British at that time. In 1878 the British gallon was legalized as 1.201 U.S. gallons. The bushel was defined as 2,150.42 cubic inches for dry measure. Bushels can be divided into the following: 64 dry pints, 32 dry quarts, or 4 pecks.

Meanwhile, in France the *quartres* and *pots* were being replaced by the metric unit of capacity, the *litre*. One gallon equals 4.546 litres.

Measuring the liquid in a container is one thing, but measuring flowing water is another. However, there is a simple and practical way of measuring flowing water in a stream or canal. That is by the use of weirs or dams to raise the water so that the flow can be controlled. One method is illustrated in Figure 9. The rate of water flow and quantity of water can be calculated by measuring the width of the slot and the head, that is, the depth of the water at the crest and the pressure at that point.

To measure water or any other liquid as it flows through a pipe, a mechanical meter is used to record the flow. There are several types. One commonly used has a rotating wheel which measures the flow in gallons a minute or gallons an hour by a direct reading counter.

4 Weight, Mass and Force

There are no historical records to show when man first used weights or invented the scale. Scales have been discovered in old graves in Egypt and Babylonia.

Ancient Babylonian weights were stones in various shapes with markings on them to show how heavy they were. The standard weight was the *mina,* believed to be the oldest weight in the world. There was a heavy mina, weighing nearly one kilogram, and a light mina that varied from .45 to .68 of a kilogram, according to the locality. The Babylonians also used the *shekel,* which was a little more than 14 grams.

The Egyptians had their *kadet,* while the Hebrews adopted the mina and shekel and also used the *talent.* They had "sacred" and "talmudist" talents and minas.

While many different systems of weights developed from early Biblical times, the western world has been most influenced by the Romans, who had two weight systems. Their smallest weight was the *uncia,* abbreviated to *oz* from which we get our word, ounce. For one system there were 16 *unciae* to one *pondus* — our pound. They also had another

Babylonian duck-shaped weight of about 60 minas which would equal about 59 kilograms.

pound, the *libra*, abbreviated to *lb* and equal to 12 *unciae*. One cubic foot of cold water equalled 60 *pondus* or 80 *libra*.

The need for scales and weights originated with bartering, just as linear measurements did. People needed some method of determining how much produce would be a fair exchange. For small products they invented the scale.

This Babylonian weight, about 4,000 years old, is approximately 7.6 centimetres high.

FIGURE 10. EGYPTIAN BEAM BALANCE

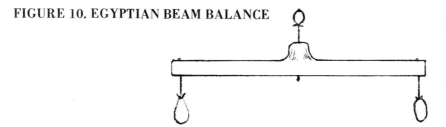

The oldest known scale, an Egyptian *beam balance*, was found when excavating a prehistoric grave. It is estimated to be 7,000 years old. From this ancient weighing device came the knife-edge equal-arm balance. The principle is a simple one: the beam rests on a knife edge so that each arm is equal and in exact balance. There are two pans, one to contain the product to be weighed, the other for the weight or weights to balance it exactly.

**French
beam balance
of 1756.**

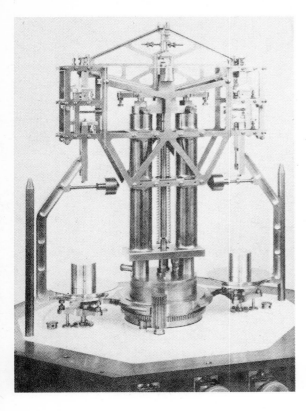

**Precision balance
with accuracies to
one part in one million.**

While complete accuracy was not essential in early-day market places, approximate weighing would not satisfy modern scientists. For them, accuracy depends on the knife edge of the balance scale being precisely in the middle. Today's laboratory equal-arm balance is extremely accurate. Yet, apart from minor scientific improvements, the modern arm balance is practically the same as that in use 7,000 years ago. Through all these centuries, the Egyptian beam balance has been in continuous use throughout the world. Merchants in Eastern bazaars still use it in its original form.

At the beginning of the first century A.D., a new principle of weighing was developed called the *steelyard* or unequal-

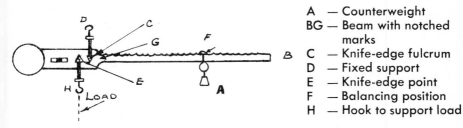

A — Counterweight
BG — Beam with notched marks
C — Knife-edge fulcrum
D — Fixed support
E — Knife-edge point
F — Balancing position
H — Hook to support load

FIGURE 11. STEELYARD

arm beam balance. The steelyard is based on a force or weight acting at a distance. For example, a 5 kilogram weight two metres from the fulcrum (the point where the beam or arm is balanced) will exactly equal a 10 kilogram weight one metre from the fulcrum or a 20 kilogram weight half a metre from the fulcrum. If notches are cut on the long arm, the weight can be moved along it to different positions to change the ratio. With the steelyard, very heavy loads can be weighed with small weights.

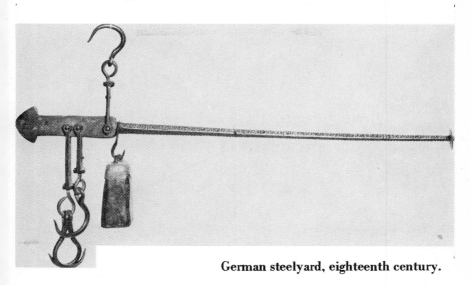

German steelyard, eighteenth century.

About 1300 A.D., when London was a centre of world trade, its merchants, influenced by the French, adopted a weight *system* called *aveir-de-peis*, an old French term meaning "weight of goods." Later it became known as *avoirdupois*, and it is still widely used as a weighing system for commerce in English-speaking countries. Ounces, pounds, hundredweights, and tons are all units of avoirdupois weight.

Hundredweights and tons came from the English. Because of the many different weights in use, King Alfred, in about 850 A.D., ordered a new container, one handbreadth to each dimension, to be filled with water. The weight of this, he decreed, would be one "measure weight" and 1,000 measure weights would be equal to one "tun weight." The "tun" was the old Anglo-Saxon word for a barrel or wine cask.

It was not long before merchants and traders found that the tun weight was too large. They preferred the measure weight or, better still, the half-measure weight, which was equal to about half a kilogram. About this time they also began to use another unit, the one hundred measure weight as an intermediate size for weighing sacks of flour, grain, or other produce. In time, the word "measure" was dropped, "tun" was changed to "ton," and the hundredweights and ton have continued in use until the present day.

In the fourteenth century there came from Troyes in France another system called *troy* weight. The troy system has always been used exclusively by jewellers for weighing gold, silver, and precious metals and is still used by them today. It includes units called grains, pennyweights, ounces, and pounds.

Apothecaries, the pharmacists or druggists of the Middle Ages, used grains of cereals on their equal-arm balances to

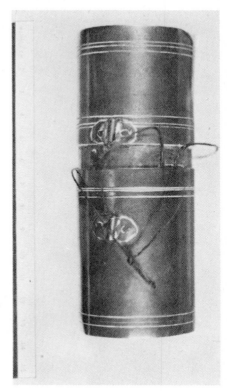

Dutch grain scale and container

weigh small quantities of drugs and herbs. The apothecaries'
main unit was, originally, a grain of wheat taken from the
middle of the ear and dried. Grains are still units of measure
— not grains of wheat, but pieces of metal. There are 7,000
grains to the avoirdupois pound and 5,750 grains to both the
troy and apothecaries' pound. The grain is the same weight in
all three systems.

   When the French adopted the metric system, they chose
the metre as their standard for length and the *kilogram* as

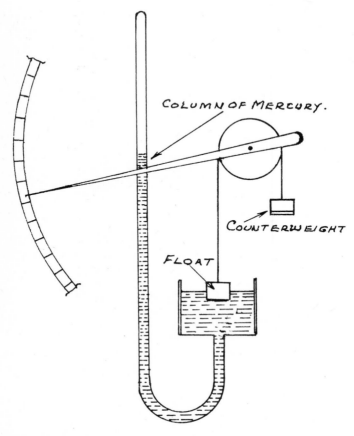

FIGURE 12. MERCURY COLUMN BAROMETER

their standard for weight. The French scientists defined the kilogram as the weight of one cubic decimetre (a cube which each side $\frac{1}{10}$ metre long) of distilled water at 0 degrees Centigrade. Although the United States has not yet officially adopted the metric system, a prototype kilogram is kept in the Bureau of Standards in Washington. The avoirdupois pound is defined by its relationship to the kilogram, just as the yard is defined in terms of the metric metre. One pound, avoirdupois, equals 0.45359237 kilogram, and one kilogram equals 2.204622341 pounds avoirdupois.

We can see the standard yard, the prototype metre or kilogram, and measure them. We can also measure a square or cube. But we cannot see weight. However, weight is related to *mass*, which can be seen, although the two must not be confused. Mass is the amount of matter in a body, whereas the weight of an object depends on the force exerted on it by gravity. Two bodies having equal masses have equal weights under identical conditions, since the earth's gravitational attraction is the same for both. Therefore, standards of mass can be used as standards of weight. A big man has more mass than a small boy and should therefore weigh more.

As there is little gravitational force on the moon — one-sixth of that on the earth's surface — an astronaut weighs less there than on earth, but the mass of the astronaut is the same as on earth. The gravitational force or pull on an object varies according to the point on the earth's surface where it is measured. Your body will weigh less on the top of a high mountain than it does in a valley or at the bottom of a deep mine. It will weigh more at the North and South Poles than at the equator. The weight of an object resting on a surface causes pressure at that point which can be measured in pounds per square foot. In the metric system it is kilograms per square metre.

Pressure of a different kind and one which we experience every day is what we call *atmospheric pressure.* Like all gases, air can be weighed, but its effect on us is variable, due to climatic conditions. Since the atmospheric pressure is constantly changing, a sensitive instrument called a *barometer* is used to measure these fluctuations. Atmospheric pressure can be measured by standing a glass tube in a bowl of mercury. The pressure of the atmosphere pushes the mercury up the tube and holds it there. By marking the tube, we can measure the pressure in terms of centimetres. At sea level, the column of mercury will be between 73.66 cm and 78.74 cm. A unit of atmospheric pressure is called an atmosphere. One atmosphere is equal to 1.03 kilograms per square centimetre or to a column of mercury 74 centimetres.

5 Time and Speed

For thousands of years men have watched the sun rise and move slowly across the sky until it sank below the horizon. We can imagine some early man seeking shelter from the noonday sun in the shade of a tree or rock and watching the shadow from his shelter moving across his body. He would notice too that the stick he carried or the spear he hunted with, when thrust upright in the ground, would also cast a shadow which would be moving in the same way over the ground. One day he would have realized that the shadow was related to the sun's movement. He may have put stones or sticks into the ground to mark where the shadow fell — and measured the movement, hour by hour.

In this way man began to understand the regularity of day-light and darkness which we call *time*. From this beginning the sundial was invented. No one knows its origin — it could have been the Babylonian astrologers, the astronomers of China or Egypt, or of some other early civilization. They all had, in one form or another, their own time-measuring instrument.

When the Sumerians adopted their numbering system with a circle of 360 degrees and a year of 360 days, they connected the two by again using the number 60. The degrees of a circle and the hours of the day were subdivided into 60 minutes and the minutes into 60 seconds. It is on this basis that time is related to the measurement of the earth's surface.

If you look at a map you will see it is divided by imaginary circular lines, or *meridians,* passing through and radiating from the earth's North and South Poles and at right angles to the equator. The prime meridian, by international agreement, passes through Greenwich, England. The measurement east or west of a fixed meridian is called *longitude.* Longitude is related to time — the difference between noon at a particular point and noon at Greenwich.

Other lines, also imaginary, run north and south of the equator and are termed *latitude.* They are used to measure

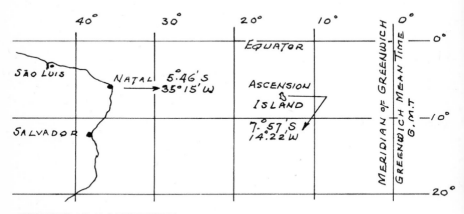

FIGURE 13. LONGITUDE

Lines of longitude west of the Greenwich meridian. Lines of latitude south of the equator.

distances from the equator. Both longitude and latitude are noted in degrees, minutes, and seconds. A designation of 8 degrees, 15 minutes, 20 seconds would be written as $8° 15' 20''$.

It is difficult to define time, but it can be measured by the rotation of the earth — around its axis, which is called a day, and as it travels in its eliptical path around the sun, a year. From this came the calendar.

Julius Caesar attempted to make the calendar agree with the solar year. He divided the year into 12 months with odd months having 31 days and even months 30, excepting February which had only 29 days. But Augustus Caesar, being born in August, thought that the month named after him should have 31 days, so he reduced February to 28 days.

Fifteen hundred years later it was discovered that the Julian calendar had resulted in a loss of 11 minutes 14 seconds every year, equivalent to a loss of 11 days. So Pope Gregory XIII, in 1582, adjusted this with his Gregorian calendar and ordered the omission of 11 days. On October 3 of that year the people of Italy, Portugal, and Spain went to bed and woke the following morning to find it was October 15. While other countries soon followed, it was not until September 14, 1752, that Great Britain and her colonies began to use the new calendar.

No two days are exactly the same length. To avoid having to change our clocks every day, an average for the year is taken and called *solar mean time* — midnight of one day to midnight of the next. By doing that we lose a number of hours each year. To make up for this loss we add one day every fourth year — known as leap year — the twenty-ninth day of February.

Mechanical clocks as we know them were first made in

Caesium atomic clock, the world's most accurate timekeeper.

Germany about the fourteenth century. In 1583, Galileo, while watching a lamp swinging in an Italian church, timed its swing and observed that although successive swings became smaller as the lamp came to rest, the time for each swing was the same. He later found that the longer the pendulum, the longer is the time of its swing. While a 6-inch pendulum swings 72 times a minute, a 24-inch pendulum swings 40 times, and a 48-inch pendulum 28 times a minute. The Dutch scientist Huygens used this principle to make the first pendulum clocks to regulate time accurately.

Early scientists divided the earth into 360 degrees of longitude. Since the earth makes one revolution in 24 hours, or 1,440 minutes, each degree of longitude is 4 minutes. It would be confusing to change the time every few miles from the prime meridian at Greenwich, so the earth has been divided into 24 standard time zones, each of one hour. Clocks are advanced or put back one hour for every variation of 15 degrees of longitude east or west of Greenwich. New York is 5 hours behind London, Berlin is 6 hours ahead of New York, and New York is 3 hours earlier than Los Angeles. Halfway around the globe, or 180 degrees from Greenwich, is the International Date Line. At this point you gain or lose one full day as you travel, depending on whether you are going east or west.

Today, with scientists demanding ever greater accuracy, the wheels and springs of the finest mechanical clocks are being replaced by atomic energy. At the laboratories of the National Bureau of Standards in Boulder, Colorado, one of the world's most accurate timekeepers has been developed. It is 20 feet long. The sicentists call it an "atomic beam spectrometer" or *caesium beam clock* because it is operated by a beam of caesium isotope 133. The first such atomic clock to be placed in regular operation was developed at the National Physical Laboratory, Teddington, England, in 1955. This clock has staked a claim to immortality for it was used in a series of experiments in conjunction with the US Naval Observatory to compare atomic and astronomical time which led ultimately to the present definition of the second as 9 192 631 770 periods of the caesium resonance frequency.

The atoms of caesium are exposed to radio waves whose frequency is maintained at an incredible speed of 9,192,631,770 cycles a second, exactly matching the natural resonance fre-

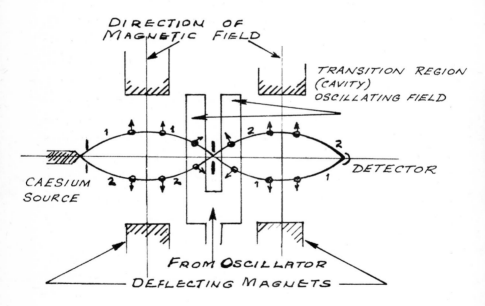

FIGURE 14. DIAGRAM OF CAESIUM ATOMIC CLOCK

The atomic beam spectrometer, showing the tuning of the oscillator to the resonance frequency of caesium atoms passing through magnetic fields and transition cavity into detector.

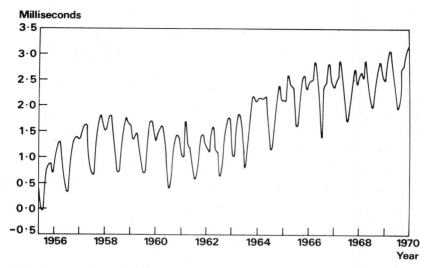

Variations in length of the day in terms of the caesium atomic clock.

quency of the caesium atoms. The frequency is maintained by a detector at the far end of the "clock". If the frequency tends to vary from the desired value, the number of caesium atoms also varies and the variation is instantly corrected by tuning an oscillator to the resonance frequency of the caesium atoms as they pass through a system of magnets towards the detector. The atomic clock is accurate to within one millionth of a second - equivalent to 1 second in 30,000 years.

Time is the key to speed, velocity, and acceleration. By relating time to distance we get speed — that is, speed equals distance divided by time. We talk of speed when driving a car, but if we travel at 30 miles per hour, that is only true if we move at a constant speed. The true measurement of speed is its velocity at any moment, or the number of feet it travels every second in one definite direction. In the metric system it is measured in metres per second. The international unit of speed is the metre per second. The velocity of a body, for scientific purposes, is its speed.

When you drive a car and increase its speed, the change in its velocity is called acceleration. The rate of change is determined by the unit of time and is measured in feet per second. Acceleration is change in velocity divided by time.

Galileo made some experiments in acceleration. Using the earth's gravitation, he discovered that two different objects, one a light weight and one a heavy weight, when released from the same height at the same time, fell to the ground at an equal acceleration; they hit the ground at the same time. The rate of acceleration is 981 centimetres per second for every second, at sea level, and is designated by the symbol G. It is especially important as a measurement in space travel.

"Supersonic" speed is the term used to indicate speed greater than that of sound. In an aircraft it varies considerably, depending on the temperature at the height the plane is flying. With a temperature of minus 60 degrees Centigrade at 50,000 feet, the speed of sound can be as low as 660 miles an hour. At sea level, on a summer's day, it is as high as 760 miles an hour. The speed at which an aircraft is travelling in relation to the speed of sound is called the *mach* number, named after the Austrian scientist of that name. Mach ½ means half the speed of sound, mach 1 is equal to the speed of sound, while mach 2 would be twice the speed of sound.

6   Electricity

Measurement indirectly created the electrical age. In 1799, Alessandro Volta assembled his voltaic electric cell which produced for the first time a flow of electricity. Except for a few scientists, no one was interested; it was just another experiment. Twenty-one years elapsed before Hans Oersted discovered a different electrical phenomenon — the electromagnetic field. Using Volta's cell, he found that when an electric current flowed through a wire, it created a magnetic field around the wire which increased in strength when the current was increased and decreased as it got weaker. But this, too, was just another laboratory event.

It was not until several more years had passed that Luigi Galvani, an Italian physicist, became interested in Volta's invention and Oersted's discovery. To him, electricity was more than an interesting experiment. Using the electro-magnetic effect, he created the first electrical measuring instrument and electricity became something tangible, something that could be used and understood. Galvani's ingenious device gave scientists the principle on which almost all

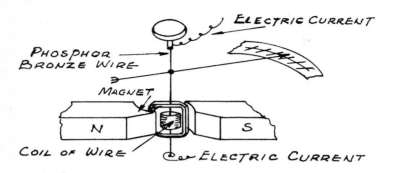

FIGURE 15. GALVANOMETER

Deflection of needle measures electric current flowing through the coil.

modern electrical measuring instruments are based.

Known as a *galvanometer,* it was very simple and very sensitive. It consisted of a small bar magnet suspended by a silk thread between two coils of fine wire through which an electric current was passed. Attached to the bar magnet was a pointer-needle which was free to move across a scale. When the current flowed through the coils, the bar magnet swung or turned in the two magnetic fields as it measured the strength of the current on the scale.

To understand how electrical measuring instruments work, one should understand something about electricity. Electricity is a natural form of energy created by the movement of electrons, which are essential parts of atoms. It is this movement or flow of electrons from atom to atom through a wire that sets up an electrical circuit. When moving along a circuit, electricity creates a magnetic field around that circuit.

Movement of electricity along a conductor such as a copper wire can be compared to water flowing through a

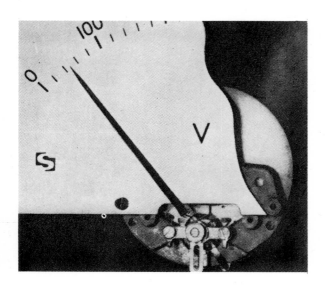

Cut-away section of moving coil ammeter-voltmeter shows magnet and pointer.

pipe. Neither will flow unless there is pressure to force it through. The roughness of the pipe slows down the water; the resistance of the metal opposes the flow of electricity.

There are three basic units of electrical measurement: the volt, the ampere, and the ohm. The *volt* is the pressure or electromotive force that makes electricity flow from one point in a circuit to another. This pressure is measured in a *voltmeter* which, like the galvanometer and other electrical measuring instruments, has a scale and a moving pointer or needle. The strength or intensity of the electric current is the *ampere.* It is the rate at which the electrons pass along the circuit and is measured by an *ammeter.*

From Galvani's basic principle of the pivoted coil of wire

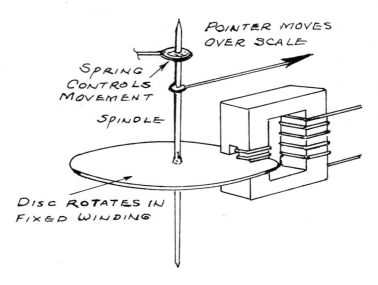

POINTER MOVES
OVER SCALE

SPRING
CONTROLS
MOVEMENT

SPINDLE

DISC ROTATES IN
FIXED WINDING

FIGURE 16. WATTMETER

For commercial use, pointer is replaced by direct reading counter to give kilowatts (units of electricity) used.

within the magnetic field of a permanent magnet came the voltmeter and the ammeter. These instruments are similar, the only difference being in the type of coils used and how they are connected in the electric circuit. Each depends on the magnetic force created and each has springs to control the swing of the indicating pointer across the scale. The accuracy of an ammeter or voltmeter depends on the size of the coil, the number of turns it contains, and the strength of the magnet. Only a small proportion of the total current flows through the measuring coil, but it is always a definite known quantity and the scale is marked accordingly.

The *ohm* is the unit of resistance, named after its discoverer, Georg Ohm, a German physicist. It was Ohm who also discovered that there was a definite relationship between voltage, current, and resistance. After many experiments and measuring what had happened, he found that voltage was always equal to current multiplied by resistance. This simple equation is useful in many ways. In a snow storm or hurricane, when an electric power line breaks, the workman has only to use his measuring instruments to find out where the trouble has occurred. Knowing that the resistance of a circuit depends on its length, once the electrician has measured the voltage and current, it is simple for him to calculate the exact spot where the line is broken.

The amount of electrical energy generated in a circuit is termed power or electrical work. The unit of electrical power is the *watt*, equal to the flow of one ampere with a force or pressure of one volt. To measure electrical work or watts, a *wattmeter* is used. This is a combination of ammeter and voltmeter. By the use of both fixed and moving coils, the whole movement becomes electromagnetic. This is the type of meter installed in homes for measuring the amount of electricity used in watt hours.

Thus, while we cannot see electricity, we are able to measure its effect and compare it to known standards for commercial or industrial use.

7   Temperature

Until early in the eighteenth century no one bothered much about temperature. In summer it was hot, in winter it was cold. There were no thermometers to measure heat. Galileo, about 1593, had made a crude one, but it was not until 1714 that the German physicist, Gabriel Fahrenheit, devised a thermometer scale with two fixed points: the temperature of melting ice at 32 degrees, and the boiling point of water at 212 degrees. He first used alcohol in the thermometer, but later replaced it with mercury.

In 1742, Anders Celsius of Sweden introduced a mercury thermometer with 100 divisions, known as the centigrade scale, from the Latin *centum,* a hundred. Celsius proposed the boiling point of water as zero and 100 degrees as the freezing point. Eight years later a colleague, Strömer, inverted this to its present form of melting ice at 0 degrees Centigrade, and the boiling point at 100 degrees Centigrade.

At about the same time, the French physicist, Réne Réaumur, suggested a third scale which ranges from 0 degrees to 80 degrees. Although still used in parts of eastern Europe, the Réaumur scale is gradually being abandoned in favour of the centigrade (Celsius) scale used by scientists, who prefer its decimal divisions.

To convert from centigrade degrees to Fahrenheit degrees, multiply by ⁹⁄₅ and add 32; to convert Fahrenheit degrees to centigrade degrees, subtract 32 and multiply by ⁵⁄₉.

Scientists have determined, theoretically, that the coldest possible point — the point where all motion of molecules ceases and there is no heat at all — is minus 273.15°C., or absolute zero. In 1848, Lord Kelvin, a British physicist, proposed a temperature scale based on absolute zero. It is limited to scientific work. By international conference, in 1948, the

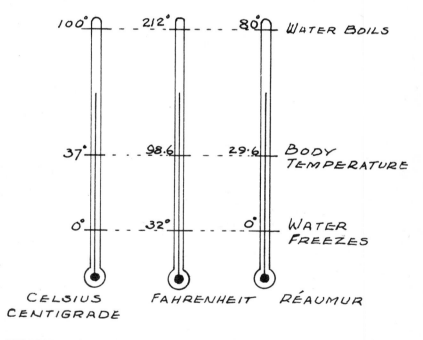

FIGURE 17. COMPARISON OF TEMPERATURE SCALES

name Celsius was adopted for the centigrade scale and the Kelvin scale was chosen as the standard temperature scale.

Heat, like electricity, is a form of energy which can be transferred from one object to another, always from the hotter to the colder. It is transferred by radiation, convection, and conduction. It is the last characteristic that is so important in measuring temperature, since conduction means that the heat is directly transferred from its source to an adjoining part with almost no loss of heat. Mercury is used in thermometers because of its quick transfer of heat. Like all metals, it expands as it gets hotter and contracts as it cools, and so rises or drops to indicate temperature degrees.

The glass thermometer, so-called because it consists of a small glass tube and a glass bulb containing the indicating liquid, is the most widely used temperature measuring device. If the temperature to be measured goes below the freezing point of mercury, then alcohol or another spirit must be used.

There are situations where the glass thermometer is not practical, however — in steel mills, refining plants, chemical

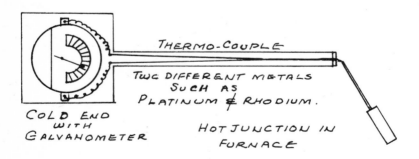

FIGURE 18. THERMOCOUPLE

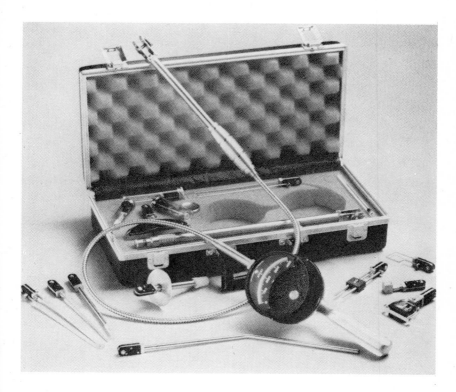

A modern thermocouple set.

manufacturing, or electric furnaces where very high temperatures are involved. For such industrial processes another type of temperature indicating instrument is used, the *thermocouple* or *pyrometer*.

A thermocouple is an electrical device that works on the basis that when two dissimilar metals, such as platinum and rhodium or copper and constantan (there are others) are joined together and the junction heated, a small electric current will flow across the junction. This current is measured by a galvanometer connected into the circuit. The

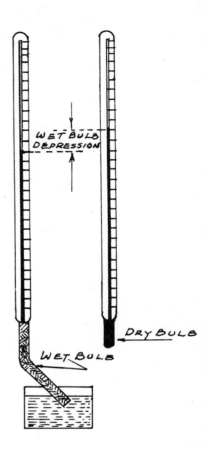

FIGURE 19. HYGROMETER

flow of electricity is shown as temperature changes and so indicated on the scale. A pyrometer is just one form of thermocouple. The best ones are very accurate. Temperatures of over 1000 degrees C. can be measured by a thermocouple.

A pyrometer — an optical one — measures temperatures by the colour of the light emitted. Metals change in colour when heated; you can see this by watching an iron bar in a fire. It will change colour as the heat is increased. Just glowing red at 440°C. changes to cherry red at 810°C. and to a brilliant

50

white at approximately 1350°C.

Life is affected not only by high and low temperatures; we are also concerned with climatic conditions. The weathermen talk of *relative humidity,* or the amount of moisture or water vapour in the air. Relative humidity is measured by a "wet and dry" thermometer, a *hygrometer.* It consists of two mercury thermometers with one bulb moistened by a saturated sleeve and the other exposed to the temperature of the surrounding air. As the water evaporates from the wet sleeve, it reduces the temperature of the wet thermometer, which is governed by the amount of water vapour in the air. The difference between the two thermometers indicates the measurement of the relative humidity as a percentage.

An important atmospheric condition is the *dew point.* Water, during the day, is evaporated by the heat of the sun. The hotter the air the more moisture or water vapour it can contain. After sunset, as the temperature drops, the reverse happens. The air cannot continue to hold its water vapour and the moisture is precipitated as dew. When this happens the ground and vegetation is covered with minute droplets of water. The measurement of the dew point is made by the use of the hygrometer, but dew point is dependent on changing climatic conditions — not only on the temperature of the air and the ground, but also on the wind and air pressure and the quantity of moisture being held by the air.

If the temperature drops below freezing, the droplets are frozen, forming the *frost point.* The measurement of dew point and frost point is of great importance to the engineer when designing air-conditioning and heating systems.

8   Light

The measurement of light — termed *photometry* — goes far back into antiquity. When man first discovered fire he used it not only for heat, but to give light to the dark interior of the caves in which he lived. After having always used torches of flaming sticks or rushes to give direct lighting, one can imagine an early man's surprise when one night a slither of blazing wood fell into a dish of fish oil or animal fat and he discovered light of a different nature — the lamp.

After those early lamps with a rush for a wick, there came a more solid form of light, a candle. No one knows when candles were first used, but the earliest candles were made of animal fat, such as tallow, with a rush embedded in it as a wick. The candle had an advantage over the lamp. It could be transported easily, measured by length and diameter, and therefore sold or bartered in the market place more readily than oil.

By the Middle Ages, when people began to regard more measurements as necessary, it was natural to seek a standard of comparison for measuring light. They decided to call the unit of light the *candle*. Men had long realized that the larger the candle the longer it would last. Two candles gave twice the light of one, three gave three times the light, and so on. It was a unit that was easy to comprehend.

We still use the candle to measure light intensity or illuminating power. It was once defined as the light from one candle weighing ⅙ pound and burning 120 grams of sperm wax. A few years ago, the unit name, candle, was changed by an international convention to *candela,* approximately equal to 0.982 of the old candle. This light intensity unit is measured when platinum is first melted and then allowed to become a solid, at what is termed the "freezing point." The light thus produced is always of the same intensity.

The brightness of light — its illuminating power, or luminous intensity, as it is called — depends on the amount of light energy emitted. Brightness has a scientific name, luminous flux, and is measured by a unit called a *lumen*. The 100-watt lamp you have in your home emits about 1,700 lumens, compared with sunlight which has a brightness equal to about 10,000 lumens.

A widely used unit of light is the *foot candle,* or lumens per square foot. It is the measurement of illumination cast by one candela intensity at a distance of one foot. In the metric system, the unit of illumination is the *lux* or metre candle. One foot candle equals 10.764 lux.

Measurement enables us to have good lighting in the home, in school, or at work. The lighting engineer, by his calculations of foot candles at the surface to be lighted, such as a desk or table, is able to design the best spacing and the right type of light fixture, the number of lamps and reflectors to give good lighting for the occupant or worker. In effect, he

**Sectional diagram
of photoelectric cell.**

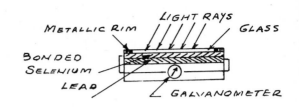

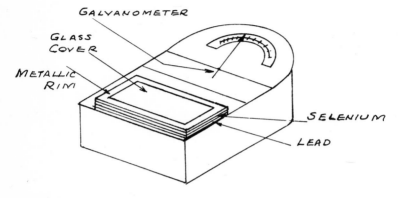

FIGURE 20. LIGHT METER

**Light meter for converting light rays into electrical energy. Used for
direct setting of cameras.**

measures the "light efficiency," or the amount of light a
lamp gives out in proportion to the electricity flowing
through it. The light efficiency of an electric lamp is
measured in "lumens per watt."

The measurement of light has been put to another and
very practical use in the *photoelectric cell* or phototube. The
photoelectric cell is based on the principle that a metal will
eject electrons when light falls on it, and cause an electric
current to flow — light energy being converted to electrical
energy. Some metals eject electrons more readily than others.
A combination of selenium and lead or copper oxide and

54

lead, in contact, will provide the circuit to make a flow of electricity possible. Such a photoelectric cell can be used as a switch, causing an electric device to operate when light stimulates the current and turning it off when the light source is interrupted. Common uses are in opening and shutting doors automatically, and for burglar alarms.

Photometers using phototubes are valuable for many purposes. The photographer's light meter is based on the phototube. The minute flow of electricity is measured by a galvanometer, but instead of indicating an electric current, it gives the correct exposure and setting for the camera.

The camera, another "light-using" device, operates by measurement. The light waves are focused through an aperture on to a photographic emulsion, called a film, to give a picture. In the simple box-type camera this is fixed, but in the more expensive cameras, the photograph depends on the

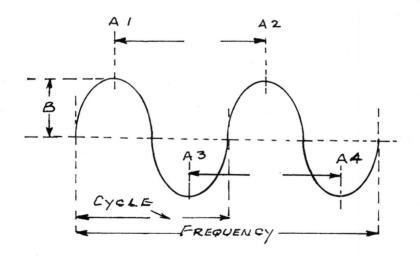

FIGURE 21. HOW A LIGHT WAVE IS MEASURED

correct measurement of the focal length of the lens and the size of the adjustable aperture, or diaphragm. The ratio of these two — dividing the focal length of the lens by the diameter of the aperture — gives an f stop setting ranging from f/1.4 to f/22. Each higher numbered f stop admits half as much light as the preceding one.

Scientists have several theories about light, but the simplest and most logical one is based on a form of wave motion. These waves flashing across space from the sun 93 million miles away are like ripples radiating outwards in ever-widening circles, rising and falling with a set frequency or rhythm, each cycle of which can be measured as the waves travel through space.

Light waves are electromagnetic in character and similar to radio waves, X-rays, and gamma-rays. While they all travel at the same velocity in space — 186,282 miles a second or almost 300,000 kilometres a second — it has been found that their lengths vary. Radio waves are long, hundreds of feet in length; the colour waves which we see in the rainbow and which scientists call the colour spectrum are much shorter: ultraviolet, X-rays, and gamma-rays are shorter still, less than one thousand millionth of an inch.

Visible light is the range of radiation — the light waves or rays of light that can be seen by the human eye. These — and they are relatively few in number — are very short in length. The violet rays of the spectrum measure four hundred thousandths of a centimetre, red rays are a little longer, seven hundred thousandths of a centimetre, with the other colour waves — indigo, blue, green, yellow, and orange — in between.

Light waves or vibrations are defined by measurements as

shown in Figure 21. Wave length is the distance between two successive similar points on the wave form, as A1 and A2, or A3 and A4. Amplitude, the variation (increase or decrease), is shown as height B. Frequency is the number of complete wave crests to adjoining troughs passing a fixed point in unit time. The period or cycle is the time taken by a wave motion to complete one vibration.

9 Sound

While the measurement of sound waves may not appear to be as important as the measurement of length, volume, weight, and other factors common to our everyday life, it has been vital in the design and development of radio, telephones, radar, and musical reproduction. These and many more inventions have depended on a scientific knowledge of sound and its transmission.

"Sound" is the term used to describe the sensation produced through the ear caused by vibrations through the air. Sound waves are like light waves, having crests and troughs. We can measure them, as we do light, by the number of sound waves or vibrations passing any fixed point. This is the *frequency*. The period of a sound wave is the time taken to complete one vibration or cyle. Thus, if the frequency is 10 per second, each period or cycle takes $\frac{1}{10}$ second.

There are limits beyond which these vibrations are not heard by the human ear. While hearing varies with the individual, the wave length of the lowest sounds audible to the average human ear is about 65 feet; the highest sounds

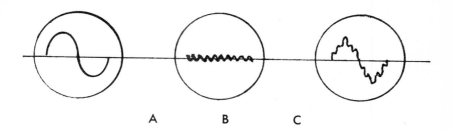

FIGURE 22. SOUND WAVES

Combination of two standard sound wave forms as seen on a cathode ray oscilloscope. (A) 100 vibrations/second; (B) 1,000 vibrations/second; (C) resultant 100 and 1,000 vibrations a second when heard together.

have wave lengths of about one inch. Sound waves below a frequency of 16 vibrations or waves a second, or above 20,000 a second, are inaudible to normal hearing. In ordinary speech, sound vibrations range from 200 to 1,000 per second.

We can study and measure sound waves by using a cathode ray oscilloscope, which is something like a television screen. In the oscilloscope a stream of electrons is directed against a flat glass screen coated with a powder that glows when and where the electrons strike it. By means of a microphone and amplifier the sound waves actually appear on the screen in the form of a wave. A standard wave is one that rises to a peak and falls to a low point and then returns to zero without any fluctuations. Other wave forms are a combination of two standard sound wave forms (see Figure 22).

When sound waves hit a wall, they bounce back or are reflected as demonstrated in the echo we hear across a mountain valley. Reflection of sound waves is utilized in several ways, at sea, in the air, and in space. At sea, the depth of the sea bed or the nearness of rocks can be accurately measured from the known velocity of the sound wave in water. Figure 23 shows how the time interval between the transmitting of a supersonic sound wave of a very high frequency and it being received back again can be used to measure the total distance it has travelled.

The speed or velocity of sound in air at ground level, at zero degrees Centigrade, is 1,090 feet per second, increasing by 2 feet per second for each degree of rise in temperature. Sound travels along a copper wire at a velocity of 10,378 feet per second.

A flash from a gun is seen from a distance but the sound of the explosion is not heard until some time later, due to the velocity of light being much higher than the velocity of sound. If the interval is timed accurately and the distance

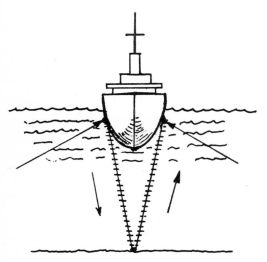

FIGURE 23.
OCEAN DEPTH-FINDING
BY SOUND WAVES

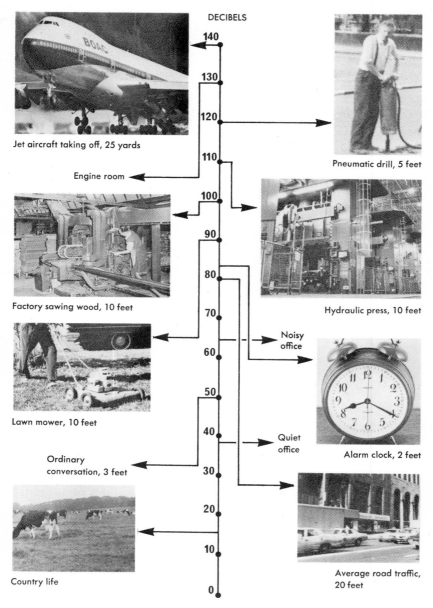

DECIBELS

Jet aircraft taking off, 25 yards

Engine room

Factory sawing wood, 10 feet

Lawn mower, 10 feet

Ordinary
conversation, 3 feet

Country life

140
130
120
110
100
90
80
70
60
50
40
30
20
10
0

Pneumatic drill, 5 feet

Hydraulic press, 10 feet

Noisy
office

Quiet
office

Alarm clock, 2 feet

Average road traffic,
20 feet

FIGURE 24. SCALE OF NOISE INTENSITY

61

known, the velocity of the sound waves can be measured. The wind, the air temperature, and the humidity (moisture in the air) can all affect the velocity of sound.

Audibility is dependent on the hearing, acute or otherwise, of the hearer. This is due to the variations in air pressure. Loudness is the intensity by which a note or sound is compared with a standard intensity. The standard intensity from which we measure loudness is taken as a frequency of 1,000 vibrations a second. The ratio of vibrations to time is defined as the unit of loudness and is called a *bel.* Since the bel is too large for common use, the *decibel,* or $1/10$ of a bel, is used. The normal ear is quick to detect any change in intensity. The decibel is to sound what the degree is to temperature. It is the magnitude of the sound and increases approximately 6 decibels each time the distance is halved.

Musical instruments produce sounds by vibrations in the air — the drawing of a bow over the strings of a violin, the air across a reed in a woodwind instrument like a clarinet or oboe, or the vibrations of the strings of a piano. The sound from an organ is due to the vibrations set up within each pipe by air blown into it at the bottom, each pipe having been made to an exact measurement of diameter and length. It is the organ builder's knowledge of measurement of sound that enables the organist, by sending air through one or more pipes, to play the music he desires.

10 Metrology

Few people have heard of *metrology* or realize how important a part it plays in everything mechanical or electrical. When we ride in our car or use any of the modern labour-saving machines in the home, switch on a motor, or listen to the roar of a jet engine in the air, we should remember that none of these could function without metrology.

Have you ever thought, when the bonnet of a car is open and you watch the engine running smoothly, what work has been done to ensure this? The valves open and shut to precise positions, allowing just the right amount of gas and air to enter. The pistons move up and down the cylinders to compress the mixture and discharge the exhaust gases. The crankshaft is turned by the power developed in the cylinders, all working in regular sequence so that the energy is transmitted to the wheels. Metal slides on metal, bearings support rotating shafts, timing devices flash a spark at the right moment. Everything functions to perfection, or as near to perfection as is possible, because hundreds of small parts you cannot see have been measured to thousandths, often millionths, of an inch. All this is due to metrology, the science of accurate measurement.

Look at your bicycle as the wheel revolves around a central hub. Ball bearings must fit, neither loosely nor tightly. The wheel must run easily and smoothly, allowing only space enough for a thin film of oil. If it were too tight the wheel would not revolve.

No matter how expert a mechanic is, his skill is limited by the equipment he uses and his tools. To ensure satisfactory results he has to check his work with gauges or specially designed measuring apparatus.

In these days, metrology has come to mean the use of extremely fine measurement in the design of moving parts for almost all machinery and apparatus. Metrology is the scientific adaptation of length, width, volume, weight, and so on, to a precise degree. Fine workmanship is the expert use of tolerance to cover reasonable imperfections. Tolerance is the difference between the high and low limits of size for a specific dimension.

Metals, as we know, expand when heated and contract when cooled. Thus, when different metals are used in any piece of equipment — an engine, for instance — temperature changes become vitally involved. It should be remembered that for every 10 degrees of difference in temperature there will be the following changes:

Steel	60 millionths of an inch
Aluminium	130 millionths of an inch
Brass	90 millionths of an inch

These changes must be reckoned with in the design and use of moving parts.

Paul Vernier invented the device that bears his name, the *vernier,* which gave instrument makers a small movable scale for measuring fractional parts or subdivisions of a larger, fixed scale. About the same time, in 1638, Gasgoigne, an astronomer, invented what he called a *micrometer* to measure the images of stars seen in his telescope. But extreme accuracy was not possible until James Watt in 1772 made his micrometer with a movable arm that could be moved in a slide by means of a screw engaging a rack. The accuracy of the pitch of the screw-thread enabled him to read divisions on a dial to one-thousandth of an inch.

By using a combination of a caliper (which has a pair of sliding jaws) and a vernier scale, it is possible to measure the thickness of an object, or the diameter of a cylinder — its exterior or interior.

For finer measurement, with accuracies of thousandths of an inch or higher, a modern micrometer must be used. This consists of two scales, one on the barrel and one on the thimble. While each division on the barrel equals twenty-five thousandths of an inch, a division on the thimble is one-thousandth of an inch. By rotating one in relation to the other, the two inter-relating scales give an extremely accurate dimension.

In the inspection of round machined parts, such as crankshafts, pistons, and cylinders, instruments are needed to measure roundness and smoothness and to make sure the alignment is true. It has been found that shafts sometimes become oval over a period of time so that it is necessary during maintenance checks to see that shafts are perfectly

Direct reading micrometer.

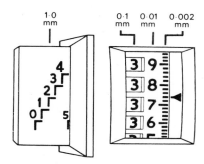

Enlarged view of sleeve and thimble showing a metric reading to two thousandths of a millimetre.

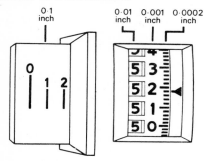

Enlarged view of sleeve and thimble showing inch reading to two ten-thousandths of an inch.

round. Cylinders also have to be checked, both inside and out, for the same reason.

Where extremely fine limits of measurements are vital, as in the manufacture of optical devices or equipment for the aircraft industry or space projects, calibrations may have to be as close as one-millionth of an inch to ensure perfection in the finished product. For this there are gauges and gauge blocks with minute variations. Some sets of gauge blocks have as many as a hundred pieces with over 100,000 different gauging dimensions, varying by infinitesimal sizes. Such gauges must be kept in dust-free rooms with temperature and humidity carefully controlled.

Smoothness is another essential when one flat object has to slide over another. To check or measure uneven surfaces, which the eye cannot see or the touch feel, an instrument called a *comparator* will measure and record inaccuracies by means of a pointer travelling along a scale. Very small movements are magnified to a high degree of precision. The

James Watt's micrometer, forerunner of today's instrument. It measures 6 inches by 5 inches.

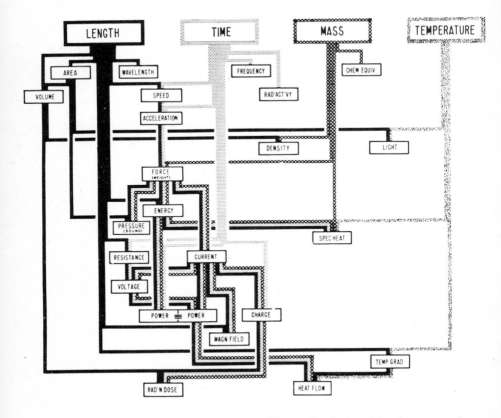

Genealogy of a measuring system. Typical relationships between the many systems of measurement.

magnification can be as much as 3,000 times and give accurate readings of 5 millionth of an inch. There are other precision machines for measuring to within one-hundred-thousandth of an inch when checking the diameter and external threads and pitches of screws.

In these days of mass production, it is not enough to have only reasonably accurate measurement. Workmen must be

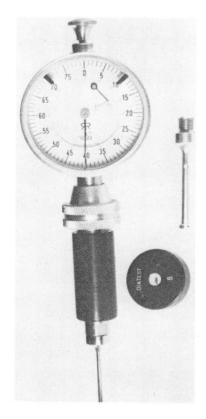

Diatest gauge for small bore measurement.

able to produce component parts that can be interchangeable
in assembly or used later for replacements.

11 Measurement in Space

Space, the interstellar cosmos around us, is so vast that even by measurement we are unable to visualize what is meant by the term. We can only begin to understand, and then but vaguely, the distance involved when we contemplate our own solar system with its own planets constantly moving in calculated eliptical orbits. Yet the axiom "to measure is to know" is not only true on earth, it is also true in space, especially when we are dealing with celestial bodies comparatively near to us.

Our solar system is only a very small part of one colossal galaxy of stars, dust clouds, and gases which we call the Milky Way. Because we are in it, it is hard for us to envisage our own galaxy. And there are millions of galaxies within range of our telescopes, some very much like our own, others of even greater immensity.

Measurement tells us that light travels at a speed of about 186,000 miles a second. To get a simpler understanding of this and the incredible distances involved, astronomers use a unit of measurement, the *light year*. One light year means

Astronaut with lunar measuring instruments.

that a ray of light has travelled 6 million million miles in one
year. To realize what this means to us on earth, if the light of
one of the most distant stars of our own galaxy, the Milky
Way, suddenly ceased, we would not know it for several years
to come.

The moon has been the centre of scientific curiosity for centuries. We know that the mean distance of the moon from the earth is approximately 238,850 miles. We know its exact orbit, but until the first astronaut landed on the moon, we knew little else; it was mere guesswork. The instruments left by the astronauts of Apollo 11, Apollo 12, and subsequent missions will, it is hoped, give us the answers to the many questions asked by the space scientists.

Deployment of lunar measuring instruments (see Figure 25).

ALSEP (Apollo Lunar Surface Experiments Package) was to have flown on Apollo 11. Because of time and distance problems, the Early Apollo Scientific Experiments Package (EASEP) was deployed instead. It could be placed seventy feet from the lunar module in about ten minutes.

The first instrument to function on the moon's surface was the *seismometer* left by the astronauts of Apollo 11. Its main purpose was to record and measure lunar rumblings and movements. Were there moonquakes, tremors, that would indicate if the interior of the moon was still a hot, volcanic mass like the earth, or a cold, dead sphere? The seismometer is so sensitive that it immediately recorded the astronauts' movements, the tread of their feet, the impact of articles placed carefully on the moon's surface. It has recorded seismic activity and rock slides down the sides of nearby craters. The seismometer on the moon is only 11 inches in diameter and 15 inches high, but its sensors are extremely sensitive.

Another measuring instrument from Apollo 11 to send reports back to earth gave the constantly changing surface temperature. On the third lunar day after the astronauts left the lunar surface, which began on September 16, 1969, signals were received indicating a temperature at one place on the moon of minus 52 degrees F. in the early dawn. At another place, the shadowed west-facing solar panel of the instrument reported a temperature — at the same time — of minus 242 degrees F. The maximum temperature of the solar cells on the dust detector during the first lunar day was over 210 degrees F. So it seems that temperatures on the lunar surface could well range from minus 300 degrees F. in the night to plus 250 degrees F. during the day.

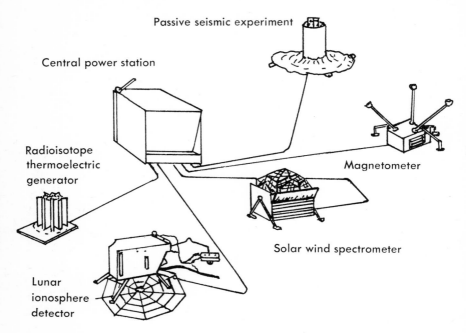

Passive seismic experiment

Central power station

Radioisotope
thermoelectric
generator

Magnetometer

Solar wind spectrometer

Lunar
ionosphere
detector

FIGURE 25. APOLLO 12 LUNAR SURFACE EXPERIMENTS

Figure 25 shows where the ALSEP instruments of Apollo 12 were placed. One was the *solar wind spectrometer.* Space scientists tell us that the sun gives off a constant flow of charged particles called the "solar wind," together with light and heat. The effect of this wind on the moon, the number of charged particles striking its surface, the energy, velocity, direction, and other data will be measured by the spectrometer. It is 17 inches high, 11 inches long, and 9 inches wide, and weighs about 12 pounds. It requires only 6½ watts to operate it.

The lunar *magnometer* with its three very sensitive devices, called sensors, measures the magnitude and direction of the surface magnetic field of the moon. It is not thought to be strong, but the effect of the solar wind may create lunar magnetic fields and divulge the moon's conductivity. This may tell us if there are deposits of iron or other metals in the moon's interior.

Two other instruments were left on the moon. There was the *lunar atmosphere detector,* to measure the pressure and density of the lunar atmosphere. It weighed about 12½ pounds and took only 6½ watts of operating power. The *lunar ionosphere detector* measures the flux, density, velocity, and energy in the vicinity of the lunar surface. It stands on a wire mesh ground screen.

The electric power to operate all these instruments is generated by and distributed from a central atomic power assembly using the nuclear fuel, plutonium 238.

The scientific world will now be aided by a wide selection of accurate measuring instruments placed in different locations on the moon's surface by the astronauts, beginning with Apollo 11 and augmented by all the subsequent landings up to the present time.

What will all this mean to us on earth? For the present we do not know, but since Galileo made his first telescope, man has been striving for a greater knowledge of space. We hope that through measurement, lunar scientific research will provide us with a better understanding of solar activity and its effects on life on the earth, information which the earth's atmosphere and the radiation zones and magnetic fields several hundred miles above the earth prevents. Scientists also hope to discover with lunar measuring instruments if minerals which are scarce on earth or unavailable here exist on the lunar soil.

Scientists, physicists, oceanographers, and meteorologists are constantly using their instruments to measure phenomena on land, in the sea, and in the atmosphere. By every known device, in different parts of the world, results are continually compared. Science knows no barriers. With measurement we will know.

TABLE OF COMPARISON

	Imperial		*Metric*	
Length	0.3937	inch	1	centimetre
	39.37	inches	1	metre
	0.621	mile	1	kilometre
	1	inch	2.54	centimetres
	1	yard	0.9144	metre
	1	fathom (6 feet)	1.8288	metres
	1	furlong (660 feet)	201.16	metres
	1	mile (5,280 feet)	1609.34	metres
Volume	1	cubic inch	16.387	cubic centimetres
	1	cubic foot (1728 cu. in.)	0.0283	cubic metre
	1	cubic yard (27 cu. feet)	0.7646	cubic metre
	1.3079	cubic yards	1	cubic metre
Area	1	square inch	6.452	square centimetres
	1	square foot	929.03	square centimetres
	1	square yard	0.8361	square metre
	0.155	square inch	1	square centimetre
	1550	square inches	1	square metre
Capacity	1	gallon	4.546	litres
	0.22	gallon	1	litre
	0.88	quarts quarts	1	litre
	1.76	pints art	1	litre
Weight	2.2046	pounds, avoirdupois	1	kilogram
	1	pound, avoirdupois	0.4536	kilogram
	1	liquid quart	0.946	litre
	1	U.S. gallon	3.785	litre

77

Index

79

ACKNOWLEDGMENTS AND CREDITS

THE AUTHOR is indebted to Jon Eklund, Curator of Chemistry, Smithsonian Institution; Arthur Schach of the National Bureau of Standards, Washington, D.C.; Ferenc Gyorgyey, Historical Librarian, Yale University School of Medicine; Mrs. P. Anderton, National Physical Laboratory, Teddington, England; J.I. McKenzie, Sifam Ltd., J.E. Curtis, Research Assistant, British Museum, London; Gladys and Elan Lieberg, Washington, D.C.; and to many others for their generous co-operation and invaluable assistance.

£2.80

TELEPEN

17283111